Cones

BY NANCY FURSTINGER

The Child's World

Published by The Child's World®
1980 Lookout Drive • Mankato, MN 56003-1705
800-599-READ • www.childsworld.com

Acknowledgments
The Child's World®: Mary Berendes, Publishing Director
Red Line Editorial: Editorial direction
The Design Lab: Design

Photographs ©: Shutterstock Images, cover (left), cover
(bottom right), 1 (left), 1 (bottom right), 3 (left), 5,
6, 10, 12; Valdis Torms/Shutterstock Images, cover
(center), 1 (center), 9; M. Unal Ozmen/Shutterstock
Images, cover (top right), 1 (top right), 3 (right),
14; Getty Images/Thinkstock, 4; Thinkstock, 15;
Bruce Raynor/Shutterstock Images, 17; Constantine
Androsoff/Shutterstock Images, 18; Le Do/Shutterstock
Images, 20; Kotenko Oleksandr/Shutterstock Images,
21; Andrey Cherepanov/Shutterstock Images, 22

ISBN 9781623239817
LCCN 2013947240

Printed in the United States of America
Mankato, MN
November, 2013
PA02194

ABOUT THE AUTHOR

Award-winning author Nancy
Furstinger enjoys searching
for inspiring shapes in nature
as she hikes with her big
pooches. She is the author of
more than 100 books.

CONTENTS

WRITING WITH ICING

You baked a delicious cake for your friend's birthday. Now you need to decorate it. You fill up an icing tube with chocolate icing. You slowly squeeze the icing out of the pointy tip and write your friend's name.

Some icing tube tips can make wavy lines or star patterns.

Now your cake is ready for the birthday party! Don't forget to pass out the party hats so everyone can celebrate.

Did you notice how the shape of the icing tube tip matches the shape of the party hats? Both of these shapes are **cones**.

Blow into your noisemaker. It's a cone with the tip cut off.

How many cones can you count in this picture? Cones have length, width, and height.

WHAT DOES A CONE LOOK LIKE?

Cones are all around us. Cones are shapes that have three **dimensions**. They aren't flat. Shapes that are flat, like a circle, have only two dimensions: length and width. These flat shapes are also called plane shapes or 2-D shapes.

Shapes like cones that have three dimensions are called **3-D** shapes. We can measure all three dimensions of a cone: length, width, and height. 3-D shapes are also called solid shapes.

How can we recognize a cone? Look closely. A cone has a flat, round bottom called a **base**. If you trace around the cone's base, you draw a circle!

The flat circle forms one **face** of the cone. A face is a two-dimensional flat **surface**.

Each cone has a curved surface as well. The cone's curved surface wraps around the circle. This curving side forms an **edge** where it comes together with the circular base. The curved surface also forms a corner that is shaped like a point. This corner is called a **vertex**.

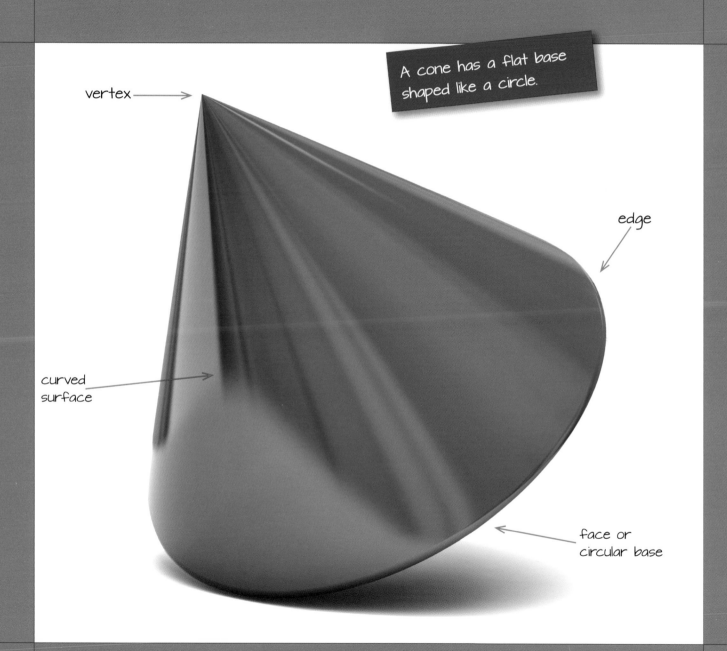

vertex →

A cone has a flat base shaped like a circle.

edge

curved surface

face or circular base

CONES AT WORK

Once you know what a cone looks like, you can easily spot this 3-D shape. You'll start to see cones everywhere.

Look out! There's a gigantic pothole! Bright orange-and-white striped traffic cones mark the spot. When people see these cones, they know to drive carefully.

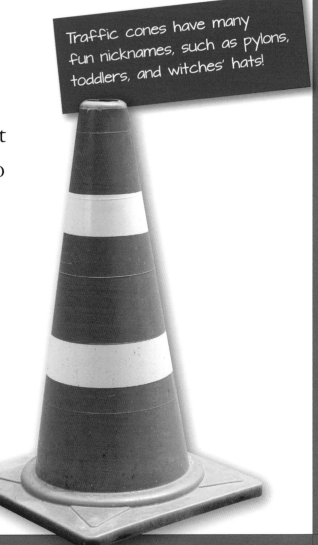

Traffic cones have many fun nicknames, such as pylons, toddlers, and witches' hats!

The earliest traffic cones were made of concrete. Today plastic cones bounce back if they're run over. Traffic cones come in other colors, but orange is most popular.

Cone Art

The artist Dennis Oppenheim created five gigantic traffic cones. He displayed them in Seattle's Olympic Sculpture Park. He named these giant pieces of art "Safety Cones." The bright orange fiberglass cones stand 18 feet (5.5 m) high. That's as tall as a giraffe!

CONES AT PLAY

Your class is putting on a play. You volunteer to help build the scenery. Your castle rises tall and straight. Your friend tells you to add a tower. You crown the tower with a cone. Now you've built a splendid castle!

The princess in the play wears a hat in the shape of a cone. This cone-shaped headdress became popular with noble women in the Middle Ages.

Stiff cloth formed the frame, which was covered with silk. A see-through veil floated down the back. Some headdresses stood 3 feet (1 m) high. They were so tall that women had problems walking through doorways!

Turrets

The cone-shaped towers soaring high above castles are called turrets. Turret comes from a French word meaning "small tower." These tiny towers rise straight up from the walls of castles. In the Middle Ages, armies used them as a lookout point to watch for approaching enemies. Today turrets are used for decoration.

ICE CREAM CONES

The most famous cone holds scoops of ice cream. Double-decker scoops don't dribble all over our hands when they're in a cone!

We can choose a sugar cone, a wafer cone, or a waffle cone. Fancy cones are dipped in chocolate. Then they're rolled in candy sprinkles or nuts.

Machines in factories can make 150,000 cones every day. Imagine how much ice cream would be needed to fill that many cones!

Ice cream in a cone is a delicious treat!

First Ice Cream Cone

The first ice cream cone was invented in New York City in 1896. Another version of this tasty ice cream holder appeared at the 1904 Saint Louis World's Fair. When an ice cream seller ran out of dishes, a man selling waffle pastry had an idea. He rolled a waffle into a cone shape. Problem solved!

LIVING IN A CONE

Some people lived in cone-shaped tents. Native Americans who roamed the Great Plains until the 1800s brought along their portable homes called tepees. Tepees offered Native Americans a snug and weather-tight home.

Ten to 20 poles gave the tepee its cone-shaped structure. Then it was covered with buffalo or elk hides. An opening at the top and smoke flaps allowed people inside the tepee to cook over an open fire and stay warm.

The cone-shaped tents were easy to take apart. The bundle of hides and poles was easy to drag.

At first, the Native Americans used dogs to help move their homes from place to place. Later, when horses arrived on the Plains, Native Americans switched to horsepower. Since horses were stronger, they could drag longer poles. Tepees rose higher, up to 20 feet (6 m) tall, or about the height of five children.

Modern-day tepees are covered with cloth. Now they last longer and are lighter. Tepees are the perfect shelter for camping!

A tepee is a cone with a door and a flap to let campfire smoke out.

The wind lifts up a windsock so you can tell how hard the wind is blowing.

CATCHING WIND IN A CONE

What type of cone shows you which direction and how fast the wind is blowing? It's a windsock, which got its name because it looks like a giant sock. The windsock is attached to the top of a pole, like a flag. When wind fills the windsock, it takes on the shape of a cone. The windsock droops if the wind is low. The windsock flies **parallel** to the ground if the wind is high.

Windsocks soar with the speed of wind at airports and alongside windy spots on highways. People also decorate their yards with bright windsocks.

CONES IN NATURE

You can find cone shapes in nature. Some colorful cone-shaped flowers rise on stalks. Many pine trees are shaped like cones. Their woody pinecones are named for their shape. They produce seeds from which new pine trees grow.

Most volcanoes form cone-shaped hills when they erupt. Two types of volcano cones are common.

Pine trees are wide and round at the bottom and grow high to a point.

Cinder cones form when hot molten rock called lava is blown out of the volcano's vent, or opening. The tiny bits of lava look like cinders. Composite cones form after dramatic explosions. They are made up of layers of ash, lava, and broken rock.

Some mountains are shaped like cones.

Search for cone shapes wherever you go. You'll be amazed how many of these 3-D shapes you can discover in your house or out and about!

HANDS-ON ACTIVITY: CREATE A CLOWN HAT

This cone-shaped hat is fun and easy to make. You can decorate your hat any way you want to!

Materials

- Colored construction paper
- compass
- pencil
- scissors
- stapler
- glue
- stickers
- pompom

Directions

1. Use a compass to draw a half circle on construction paper. The half circle should be about 20 inches (50 cm) across.
2. Cut out the half circle.
3. Roll the shape into a cone.
4. Staple the cone at the base of the seam. Try the hat on and adjust if necessary. Then glue the seam shut. Remove the staple when the glue is dry.
5. Decorate your clown hat with stickers. Top it with a pompom.

GLOSSARY

base (BASE): A base is one of the flat surfaces of a 3-D shape. The base of a cone is a circle.

cones (KOHNS): Cones are 3-D shapes with circular bases that slope up to a point. Ice cream cones and birthday hats are two examples of cones.

dimensions (duh-MEN-shuns): Dimensions are the length, width, or height of an object. A cone's height is one of its dimensions.

edge (EJ): An edge is the line where a surface begins or ends. A cone's edge is where the circular base meets its curved side.

face (FASE): A face is a flat surface on a 3-D shape. A cone's face is also its base.

parallel (PAR-uh-lel): Lines that are parallel are always the same distance apart. A windsock flies parallel to the ground when the wind blows hard.

surface (SUR-fis): A surface is the flat or curved border of a 3-D shape. A cone's curved surface rises to a point.

3-D (THREE-DEE): A 3-D shape has three dimensions, length, width, and height. A 3-D shape is not flat.

vertex (VUR-teks): A vertex is the point where the edges of a 3-D shape meet. A cone has one vertex at its point.

BOOKS

Cohen, Marina. *My Path to Math: 3-D Shapes*. New York: Crabtree Publishing Company, 2011.

Hoban, Tana. *Cubes, Cones, Cylinders, & Spheres*. New York: Greenwillow Books, 2000.

WEB SITES

Visit our Web site for links about Cones: *childsworld.com/links*

Note to Parents, Teachers, and Librarians:
We routinely verify our Web links to make sure they are safe and active sites. So encourage your readers to check them out!

INDEX